Beachlers Guide to Vehicle Care and Repair

Automotive Basics from Fluids to Flats

ISBN: 978-1-964046-01-3

Brett Beachler, Vice President
Beachlers Vehicle Care & Repair
3623 North University at War
Memorial Drive
Peoria, Illinois 61604-1393
www.Beachlers.com

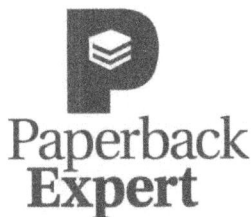

Paperback
Expert

www.PaperbackExpert.com

❦❦❦❦❦❦

Dedication

This book is dedicated to all the folks seeking to educate themselves on vehicle maintenance and repair—what to do and what NOT to do! This "education" will enable you, the vehicle owner and operator, to make informed decisions on vehicle repair, maintenance, and purchasing.

❦❦❦❦❦❦❦

Acknowledgements

First, I would like to thank God for all of His blessings and provisions and for allowing us to serve our community since 1951. We can only serve others and enjoy life because of His creation and the forgiveness He has given us in Jesus Christ.

My wife, Rebecca, is my "pillar" who makes it possible for me to devote my work time and energy to the business. It is because of my wife that I am able to lead and serve to the best of my ability. She and our children make the hard work worthwhile!

I want to thank my dad, Terry Beachler, who has been instrumental in my life and this business. As in many family businesses, there will always be "challenges" we face. There are often times in life when parents and

Brett and Terry Beachler

children do not agree. However, we continue to press forward to ultimately improve our customers' experience. I also want to thank my mom, Barbara, for instilling in me the fundamental nature of "taking care of people." Without the influence of my mother's guidance and tact, I would not be where I am today.

I appreciate each member of our staff because this business would not succeed without their efforts and dedication. We have highly skilled and experienced technicians at Beachlers, and each one contributes positively to our effort.

I am grateful to our customers. They are some of the greatest customers in our industry. We are thankful that many of our new clients have come for service because of a recommendation from one of our current customers. The greatest compliment our business can receive is the referral of a customer to Beachlers. It is truly an honor.

Testimonials and Customer Reviews

"Thank you, thank you, thank you. By the way, you now have a super fan in my wife, Susie. She just called me singing your praises. She will be telling everybody about Beachlers. She now understands why I rave about Beachlers. You guys rock. Thanks again, Brett."

— Mark K.

"Just know that you and your staff are amazing. I am almost 80, but I know I have great trust in you and all your staff. You may not know how important that is (I think you do…you have been guided by your great family). You guys are about as good as it gets…I am thrilled to be your customer and friend. Your kindness and professionalism are TOPS!"

— Mary V.

"Brett, just arrived in New Jersey. The car ran great and no issues with the tires. Thanks for your great attention to details and finding the engine mount problem before we left. Your professionalism is why all of our family have our cars worked on at your station."

— Ron S.

"Brett, it all started with a warm welcome to the neighborhood from you guys. Then you and your team went above and beyond servicing my vehicle. I find pleasure in supporting local businesses, and I know others do, too. Which is why I will refer you to my friends and family at any chance. Best to you and I am sure I will see you down the road (pun intended)..."

— JD D.

"Thank you so much for your honesty, integrity, and especially your expertise. Twice now you have gotten me safely back on the road and I have never wondered whether I had been "taken for a ride." I will always come back to Beachlers!"

— Jillian R.

"I especially appreciated Brett stopping by the hospital and picking up the vehicle to replace the tires. It had been an especially busy week and I did not know when I could have gotten it done without this help. I wanted to have the tires installed as soon as possible before the first snow. The tires were getting pretty dangerous."

— John P.

"Service was above and beyond! Got us in right away, always friendly, professional, and they followed up to make sure everything worked out!"

— Angie V.

"After multiple trips to the manufacturers/dealer's own service center (which could not identify/fix the noise), Beachlers resolved the problem and fixed it! Great service, respectful staff, and love the text updates!"

— Mike B.

"Appreciate the 'trip check' service. Makes me feel a lot better about a car with 140,000 miles on a road trip. Thanks for the reasonable price, too."

— Judy M.

"You guys did a really great job doing what I asked. Your inspection of my car blew me away. So many places do offer the inspection. But do not do as good of a job. I look forward to returning to do more business with you. I really like it that I can drop off my car and pick it up as late as 9:30 pm. I have a big family and a very busy lifestyle. Keep up the good work."

— Kristopher H.

"We have been going to Beachlers for 36 years--they are what everyone seeks, but is so hard to find: a trusted auto repair shop."

— Sheldon S.

"I think that no one has come close to matching the service, ease of making appointments, and the willingness of the staff to offer advice or recommendations upon being asked."

— Dave H.

"Fast, friendly service sounds cliché, but that describes my experience perfectly. I am so appreciative to have a solid go-to repair shop so near and so well-equipped to handle my vehicle repair needs."

— Amy B.

And a final testimonial that needs no words, beyond telling you that this vehicle has over 241,000 miles on the odometer…and showing you the big smile on the owner's face!

Table of Contents

CHAPTER 1: WHY I WROTE THIS BOOK.................................... 1
CHAPTER 2: STEPPING INTO THE FAMILY BUSINESS 5
CHAPTER 3: OUR GUIDING PRINCIPLES................................. 9
  OUR PHILOSOPHY 9
  COMMUNICATION AND TRUST 10
    Education 10
    Transparency 13
    When Less Work Is More Service 14
CHAPTER 4: OUR SHOP 17
  OUR FACILITIES 17
  OUR EMPLOYEES 19
  CUSTOMER SERVICE 19
  CUSTOMER INCENTIVES 21
CHAPTER 5: CAR CARE 101 23
  LEARNING THE LINGO: ACRONYMS 23
    ASE = Automotive Service Excellence 24
    ABS = Anti-Lock Brake System 25
    AT = Automatic Transmission 26
    BCM = Body Control Module 26
    CSS = Cooling System Service 26
    DIS = Driver Information System 27
    EGR = Exhaust Gas Recirculation 27
    LOF = Lube, Oil and Filter Service 27
    PCM = Powertrain Control Module 28
    TPMS = Tire Pressure Monitoring System 28
    TPS = Throttle Position Sensor 28
  DASHBOARD: LIGHTS THAT POP UP 29
    ABS Light: 30
    Check Engine Light: 31
    Oil Light: 31
    Reduced Power Light: 33
    Smart Air Bag Light: 34
    SRS Light: 35
    Temperature Light: 35
    Traction Control Light: 36
  DASHBOARD GAUGES 37
    Battery Gauge: 38
    Fuel Gauge: 39
    Odometer: 40
    Speedometer: 40

Tachometer: *40*
Temperature Gauge: *41*
NOISES 43
Brake Squeaking *44*
Brake Grinding *45*
Squeaky Engine *45*
Thumping While Turning *46*
Thumping While Driving *47*
Whining Engine *48*
Vehicle Starting *49*
ENGINE OIL 49
Oil service Frequency *51*
CHAPTER 6: CAR CARE 201 ....**53**
SHOULD YOU BUY A NEW CAR? 54
EXTENDED WARRANTIES 56
CARING FOR YOUR CAR 57
PREMIUM FUEL 58
MOTOR CLUB MEMBERSHIPS 59
CHAPTER 7: INTRODUCTION TO MAINTENANCE **61**
VEHICLE FLUIDS 62
Transmission Fluid *62*
Differential Fluid *62*
Power Steering Fluid *63*
Brake Fluid *63*
Cooling System Fluid: Antifreeze/Coolant *63*
Air Conditioning System Fluids/Refrigerant *64*
TESTING AND DIAGNOSIS 65
CHAPTER 8: CAR CARE 301 ....**67**
YOUR AUTOMOTIVE "HOW TO" GUIDE 67
How to Change a Flat Tire *67*
HOW TO JUMP-START A CAR 70
HOW TO MANAGE A BREAKDOWN 72
HOW TO MANAGE AN ACCIDENT 73
HOW TO MANAGE BEING STUCK IN TRAFFIC 75
HOW TO DRIVE ON SNOW AND ICE 76
HOW TO BUY A USED CAR 77
HOW TO FIND A GOOD REPAIR SHOP 80
Five Questions to Ask a Shop *82*
APPENDIX I: EXTENDED WARRANTIES **83**
APPENDIX II: FUEL TIPS AND TALES **87**
ABOUT THE AUTHOR **91**
NOTES **93**

CHAPTER

1

WHY I WROTE THIS BOOK

Designed to replace the horse, the automobile was originally called the "horseless carriage." It has succeeded in its original goals, getting us where we want to go faster than horses ever could and making our work much easier.

I remember when each car seemed to take on the owner's personality. And when a car was coming toward you, you knew exactly what make and model it was—there were not that many possibilities! Certainly nowhere near the many different nameplates and hundreds of different models we have now, made even more difficult by the number of years cars stay on the road these days.

Technology is advancing so rapidly that a complete understanding of your car is nearly impossible, unless you live and breathe it. People say they used to be able to look under the hood and name every part they saw. Today those same people will not even raise the hood—they are too intimidated to look! Most of my customers say they would love to know more about their cars. That is why I wrote this book.

Serving people is my heart's desire, helping them in any way I can. If someone in need crosses my path, and I am able to help them, I do not just say, "Go be warm and be fed." Instead, I want to serve them, to help them, to meet their need, as I can.

I see a need for people to know not only how to care for their cars but to make wise choices when they replace them. So here it is—the self-help book of car ownership. It will not make you a Master Certified Auto mechanic, but it will help you better understand how to keep yourself, your family, and your car safe.

Safety is a primary objective every time we get in a car. We pray for travel mercies. We tell our children to drive safely. Road signs tell us to drive safely, to wear our seat belts, and obey traffic laws--all so that we will "arrive alive" at our destinations.

Cars were never meant to be phone booths, texting stations or music halls. They were meant to help us arrive safely.

Most of the advancements in technology have an underlying theme of safety, many of which are addressed in these pages. More importantly, this book provides simple, helpful information on car ownership. Armed with this knowledge, understanding warning signs, and knowing what to do when things go wrong will help us stay safer in and around our automobiles.

So consider me the "car dad you never had" who wants you to know how to care for your car and arrive safely. If you have a specific question, simply go to www.Beachlers.com. Let me know how I can help.

Sincerely,

Brett Beachler
Vice President, Beachlers Vehicle Care and Repair
July 2015

CHAPTER

2

STEPPING INTO THE FAMILY BUSINESS

Beachlers Vehicle Care and Repair has been a mainstay in my family and in Peoria since before I was born. My grandfather, Bob Beachler, opened the business in 1951 at the corner of North Street and McClure Avenue. Shortly thereafter, the business moved to its current location at North University Street and War Memorial Drive. The two-bay service station was out in the "sticks" then. There was only pastureland between the station and Forrest Hill a half mile to the south. War

Bob Beachler circa 1966

Memorial Drive was a one-lane street, just being widened to two lanes. Now it has four. Beachlers is no longer in the "sticks"— Peoria has grown out to meet it.

Beachlers Vehicle Care and Repair is truly a family business. My uncle Don joined the business at some point, and my dad started working there during the summer of 1959. There's a funny story about how my dad got started at Beachlers.

The story goes that he caused too much trouble around the house, so Mom sent him to work at the station. It turned out to be a great career. When my Grandpa Bob passed away in 1984, my dad took his place as the president of Beachlers.

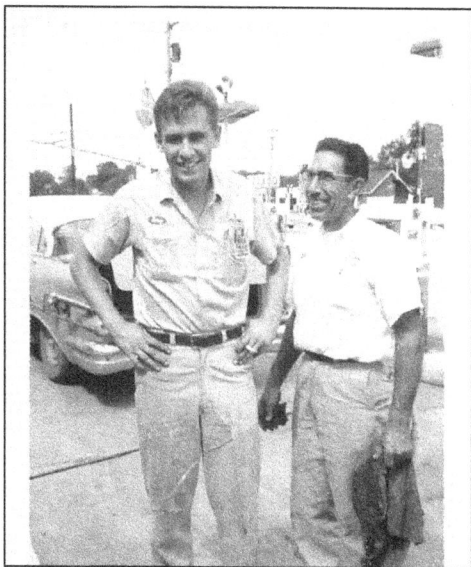

Bob and Terry Beachler in 1966

My own experience with Beachlers began when I was about 12 years old. I joined the other grandkids hanging around the shop—mowing the grass and keeping the grounds clean for income and getting the smells, the guys, and the whole atmosphere in my blood. When I turned 16 and had a choice of jobs, I chose to work here. Through high school and college, I did light duty mechanic work on cars and became very familiar with the business.

After I graduated with a four-year business degree from Bradley University, I thought I would stay here forever, but another opportunity came along. I entered the corporate world and moved to Florida, Georgia, Michigan, Colorado, and back to Peoria with one company—all in four years.

I learned a tremendous amount in that environment, but answering to a boss had run its course with me. I had really enjoyed the family business and the days of answering to a customer. Beachlers had an opportunity for me to come back, and I jumped at it. That was in 1998, and I have not looked back.

The business has doubled during this time, and I have truly enjoyed it because my passion is leading and making the business operate well. I do not mind getting dirty and I am ASE-certified as a service advisor, but the technical automotive work does not tweak my interest like it does for my technicians. I enjoy steering the ship toward our goals.

My dad plans to retire in 2016, and we have begun the transition to the third generation of Beachlers in business at this location. It may not stop there, since my youngest daughter, Katie, already has her own business card at age 12, goes to trade shows with me, and is a mini-spokesperson for the business! However, I will never pressure her in any way. I have explained, "Always give your best effort and attitude possible and you will be successful at any endeavor in life."

Three Generations: Terry, Katie and Brett Beachler

CHAPTER

3

OUR GUIDING PRINCIPLES

OUR PHILOSOPHY

Our basic philosophy is that you simply take care of people—it is really not rocket science. In our business, we exist to meet the customer's needs over the life of the vehicle, not to maximize each sales invoice.

Our mission statement is, "Provide outstanding ethical vehicle repair and maintenance through exceptional customer service while lowering the customer's vehicle's cost per mile." Implementing this philosophy takes many forms, including educating customers, honesty, transparency, and declining to perform unnecessary work—as well as providing quality automotive service.

One principle I do my best to follow and instill in our team is to view each transaction through the customer's eyes. Our natural inclination is to selfishly see our point of view. It takes an effort to resist selfishness and put on selflessness. I believe that if every employee in our organization sees through the customer's eyes, both the business and customer will be satisfied. It is difficult to do because we are always about ourselves, a bunch of sinners selfish by nature. But if you can become selfless in anything you do, you will be successful at it.

COMMUNICATION AND TRUST

Education

We want to educate you about your car so you can make sound decisions. This encompasses both the repair we are recommending and your overall care and plan for your vehicles. We do not just say, "We replaced your EGR valve." Who would automatically know what an EGR valve is? We explain what it is, what its function is, and why it needs to be replaced.

To share information that will help you take care of your car, we offer *Lunch 'n Learn* car care clinics at your business, school, or organization. We address vehicle operating expenses, proper factory specified maintenance schedules, an evaluation of extended warranties, tire information, information on inspecting a pre-owned vehicle, fuel saving tips, and a discussion of unnecessary services—which we call a "wallet flush." We also offer car care workshops each year to address maintenance questions, from what needs to be completed to what does *not* need to be completed.

We want to guide you to spend less per mile than you would have otherwise. We have calculated that during 50 years of vehicle ownership, the average you can expect to spend on a vehicle with insurance, repairs, maintenance, tires, etc., is about $431,250. The expense structure will vary based upon vehicle expense, miles per gallon, and cost of fuel. The costs that make up that total are explained below, so you can see how you may vary from the average and how you can affect your bottom line. We want to educate people on how to minimize that cost so the money can be used for what is most important to them.

EXPENSE COMPONENT	COST PER MILE
Depreciation	
(based on a $20,000 purchase price)	
75,000 mile life	26.6¢
150,000 mile life	13.3¢
250,000 mile life	8.0¢
Fuel	
30 mpg @ $3.20/gal.	10.6¢
15 mpg @ $3.20/gal.	21.3¢
Tires	
$600/60,000 miles	1.0¢
Insurance	
$1023/15,000 miles per year	6.8¢
Maintenance	
(This will affect gas mileage)	3.5¢-4.0¢

Driving an average of 15,000 miles each year for 50 years and considering the costs indicated above of approximately 57.5¢/mile, the expense is $441,750. The IRS has a mileage allowance of 57.5¢ for each business mile driven in 2015, which confirms this estimate of costs. We have numerous customers here whose cars are already paid for. They want to retain their vehicle and abstain from taking on **a** monthly car payment. Looking at the expense ratio on cars, if you keep them into the 250,000-300,000 mileage range, you are spending pennies on the mile as opposed to dimes. If you are not enslaved to car payments, you can set aside $50 or more each month for maintaining the car and obtaining those extra miles. When repairs are needed, you do not panic. You can repair the car, have a reliable vehicle, and skip the hundreds of dollars each month in car payments.

Approaching 300,000 miles and going strong

Another topic we address is how to find a quality auto repair shop. Are they AAA approved? Beachlers is the only AAA-approved auto shop in Peoria, Illinois. Are they a member of the Better Business Bureau and in good standing? Our business is. Are the technicians ASE-certified? Our technicians are ASE-certified. These certifications are independent criteria to look for in selecting a repair facility. Shops without these credentials may provide excellent service; but if you do not have another way to verify their business and mechanical integrity, meeting these standards provides that assurance. Chapter 8 in this book, "Car Care 301," provides other information to help you find a quality car repair facility should you be traveling or living in another town and need assistance.

This book is also part of the education process. The more you know about your car's needs, the better you can decide how to invest your money in maintaining your car.

Transparency

We try to be as transparent as possible for our customers to lay the foundation of trust. We are happy to give new customers a tour so they can meet our people and see the operation of our shop. Or, current customers can enter the shop bays and observe the technician working on their vehicle. Many automotive businesses do not allow customers in the work area, but our technicians are comfortable and aware of this "open door" policy. It is priceless for a customer to meet the technician working on his vehicle. Observing the procedure being performed on your vehicle can help eliminate any apprehensions you may have.

We want to be able to exhibit our operations as much as possible. We walk customers back in the shop and say, "Look at the complexity of this procedure being performed on your vehicle." Then the customer better understands the value of the service.

When Less Work Is More Service

We are not in business for the short-term sale; we are in it for the long-term customer relationship. We want to treat every customer like family. That means that we do not recommend work that is not necessary, and that may be our strongest method of building trust and demonstrating that we are working for you.

Often we are consulted for a second opinion, much like a doctor. A customer says, "I've been told I have 2.5 mm of brakes and need to replace them now. Will you measure them?" We will measure and explain that 2.5 mm is actually sufficient brake material, and we recommend replacement at 1.5 mm. At the next service interval we will re-measure the brake material. We are not in business to sell the customer brakes or other items prematurely. We now have a customer who knows they can trust that our advice is what is best for him, not us. And that is also best for us in the long term.

Occasionally it will be necessary to advise a customer that it is time to remove their vehicle from service. As a business person doing my best to serve my technicians and customers, I see a $2,000 repair estimate. But, we also are aware of another

$2,000 worth of needed repairs, and the cost/benefit for the customer does not exist. I will explain to the customer, "Based upon the needs and the value of the vehicle, it is our suggestion to sell or dispose of the current vehicle and seek another. The rust is starting and the maintenance is accumulating. Your money would be better spent by investing in another vehicle rather than repairing this one."

That does not benefit our business in the short term, but we do our best to look out for the customer's best interest. They will need repairs and maintenance on down the road to get the most miles for their money, but we will not recommend repairs that we know will not be cost-effective.

A number of automotive services are probably not needed for your car under normal conditions. These include the following:

o   Nitrogen in your tires

o   Fuel injection cleaning

o   Gas and oil additives

o   Extended warranties (see Appendix I)

o   Gas-saving contraptions

o   Power steering or brake fluid flushes

o   Oil services every 3,000 miles

o   Plugs in tires

o   Midgrade and premium fuels

o   Overzealous air filter replacement

o   PCV valve replacement

o   Ethanol in your fuel

I explain to my techs that we want our customers to have such confidence in us that we are a trusted resource. They may start as consumers, but as they grow to trust our service and advice we want them to become customers, then regular clients, and eventually our advocates. Then we have succeeded in serving them, and they in turn are our best promoters.

CHAPTER

4

OUR SHOP

OUR FACILITIES

As I have mentioned, our shop started out on the north edge of Peoria where only farms were scattered in the town. However, with the city's growth, we are now located at one of the two busiest intersections in Peoria. What began as a two-bay service station has grown to a five-bay repair center with ten gas pumps. We have a remodeled 1954 gas pump in our convenience store, which is reminiscent of those early years.

The building is still an old-style service station. However, on May 1, 2015, we opened our Vehicle Maintenance Center. This added three oil service bays, a new customer accommodation and state-of-the art waiting area. We will have the same friendly smiles, but this expansion has enabled us to

1980 Shop Crew: Terry Beachler on left, Don Beachler 2nd from left

process additional customers in a modern atmosphere.

We service domestic, Asian, and European cars as well as light trucks. We do provide service for fleets, which is a market that will be better served with our new Vehicle Maintenance Center. Our primary focus for fleet vehicles is minimizing downtime. We do everything possible to complete the service on their work vehicle the same day because that loss of transportation is lost revenue the company could be generating.

Since we sell fuel, we are also involved in that area of automotive service and expense. Information on reducing and understanding your fuel costs is included in Appendix II.

OUR EMPLOYEES

The technicians are the "brains" behind our excellent vehicle repairs and maintenance. We have five light-duty technicians who perform routine maintenance, such as oil service, tire installations, and tire repairs. These technicians are certified by the AOCA (American Oil Change Association). For the five repair and factory specified maintenance bays, we have five ASE-certified technicians who have been tested by the National Institute for Automotive Service Excellence. Our service advisors are also ASE-certified. As of 2015, the average tenure of our ASE technicians was 35 years! These technicians are invaluable to the team at Beachlers.

CUSTOMER SERVICE

Having car trouble and/or being without your car is always an intrusion in your schedule. However, we do our best to minimize the impact upon your daily life. Our new tire and oil service facility welcomes walk-in customers: no appointments are necessary in the Vehicle Maintenance Center.

In our repair bays, we schedule appointments. Generally, most vehicles with appointments are in and out on the same day. However, we know how vehicle breakdowns in the real world work, and many of our walk-in customers with some type of issue on their vehicle are handled the same day or the next day at the latest. We ask you to complete a Diagnosis Worksheet on our website. This allows our technicians to receive more accurate information regarding your vehicle's symptoms. This also can reduce evaluation time, which can save you money.

You can drop off your car as late as 9:30 PM and we provide a Night Drop-off Form on our website for you to communicate your needs to us. If you need a ride to work or alternate transportation, we have a shuttle and a limited number of loaner cars available. You can communicate with us via phone, email, or text, and we will let you know when your car is ready with the communication that is easiest for you!

When we inform you what repairs are necessary to correct the symptoms on your vehicle, our service advisors do their best to educate you about the repair. Our job is to reduce the apprehension and fear fueled by lack of information. We are here to educate and guide you in your decision-making on your vehicle's needs.

We provide "cradle-to-grave" care, so we will follow up with you personally at the proper time to let you know what factory specified maintenance and/or repairs you need to take the best car of your vehicle. That maintenance is a long-term investment to get the most miles for your dollar out of your car.

Our standard warranty on work is for two years or 24,000 miles, whichever comes first. Often a part is from a supplier such as NAPA® or AC Delco®, and they will cover the part nationwide.

CUSTOMER INCENTIVES

We value all our customers, long-time and recent additions, and plan different rewards with the opening of our enlarged facility this year. For our customers who depend upon us for all factory specified maintenance, tires, and repairs, we will provide complimentary maintenance inspections. This includes tires (pressures and condition), fluid levels, belts, exterior lights, etc. at any time. This will provide peace of mind for vehicle owners and operators.

Each month we invite a number of people who move into our area to come get to know us. We offer an oil service to these first-time customers. Instead of writing a check to Beachlers, they will write a check for the service amount or more that will be donated to our charity of choice. This will be a chance to funnel thousands of dollars each year to local needs. It will provide us the opportunity to become acquainted with new customers and hopefully develop a lasting business relationship.

CHAPTER

5

CAR CARE 101

LEARNING THE LINGO: ACRONYMS

Communication can easily break down in my industry due to the many acronyms we use. Listed here are some of the most common ones. I hope these will provide you with a knowledge base to help you make informed decisions about keeping your vehicle serviced properly.

I will give you a brief warning here: The first acronym I will discuss is ASE, Automotive Service Excellence, and it requires a lengthy explanation. Take heart! Most of the remaining acronyms are not so extensive.

ASE = Automotive Service Excellence

You will see this acronym a lot. ASE is an independent organization that tests the competency of those in our industry. ASE does not provide training; they only conduct testing and provide certification based on test results. The training takes place in other locations or through other venues, then ASE tests, much like SAT tests students preparing for college. ASE testing is administered under close supervision at a "neutral" location and the results are provided by the certifying organization.

ASE says, "We are going to see if you learned anything through what you have studied. And if you can pass our test, then we will certify that you know what you are talking about and are qualified to repair these specific systems." When someone passes their exam, they become "ASE Certified." For the automotive repair side of our industry, there are eight different areas of ASE certification. If you certify in all eight areas, you are an ASE Master Technician.

ASE also has specific certifications for diesel trucks—like a light-duty diesel truck. Additionally, they have certifications for heavy-duty diesel, certifications for people working in a parts department and certifications for service advisors.

ASE is the "gold standard" in our industry, and in my opinion, it is important that anyone who works on your vehicle should be an ASE Certified technician. Before you have any work done on your vehicle, ask if the technician assigned to your car is ASE Certified. If they are not, you may want to look for a repair shop with fully trained and certified technicians and service advisors.

ASE Certification must be renewed every five years. This is important because cars and technology change. Therefore, ASE Certified Technicians must stay up-to-date on cutting-edge technology so they can continue to service your vehicles properly. Every year there are over a million pages of new information hitting our industry, so it is important for my staff and me to stay current.

Your great-grandfather may have said all he needed to fix his car was a piece of baling wire, a pair of pliers and some duct tape. That may have been true back then, but today, we need a little more than that. That is why being ASE Certified is so important.

ABS = Anti-Lock Brake System

If you read that as a word, it says "abs." So, if we were a gym, you would think of something totally different—a part of your body. But in the car industry, ABS refers to your Anti-lock Brake System. So, if your "ABS" light comes on, that means there's a fault in the Anti-lock Brake System. (As far as your body is concerned, check with the gym on that!) If the "ABS" light is illuminated, an important safety system is not working properly!

AT = Automatic Transmission

This is the type of transmission in most passenger vehicles. In fact, it is increasingly difficult to find a standard transmission anymore. If your gearshift has choices like "Park," "Reverse" and "Drive," you have an automatic transmission. This type of transmission automatically shifts when certain conditions exist.

The invention of the automatic transmission revolutionized driving by making it much easier. Before, drivers had to use a clutch pedal and manually shift their cars into different gears, which is it is called a "manual" or standard transmission.

BCM = Body Control Module

The Body Control Module pays attention to everything internal (inside the vehicle). "Things you touch" is a simple way to define what goes through the BCM—for example, turn signals, headlights, heating and air conditioning controls and other items like these. They all send information through the Body Control Module.

CSS = Cooling System Service

CSS is our acronym for Cooling System Service. That is the process where we typically flush your cooling system and reinstall coolant. It is not a chemical flush; it is factory specified maintenance of your cooling system fluid.

DIS = Driver Information System

This system provides information to the driver. It may be an LED style display, a warning light in the dashboard console, scrolling across the dash or touch screen, or perhaps visible in a small window somewhere on the dash. You need to be aware of this important system. Pay close attention to any messages and look for more specific information and responses in the index of your owner's manual.

EGR = Exhaust Gas Recirculation

EGR is an acronym you will hear often. It stands for Exhaust Gas Recirculation. It is an emission control item and a system that recirculates exhaust gases back into the engine for re-burning. Also, fumes from your gas tank return to the engine for re-burning through this system. This promotes fuel economy and proper engine operation.

LOF = Lube, Oil and Filter Service

LOF is pronounced "loaf." What's a "loaf?" In our industry, 'LOF' means Lube, Oil and Filter. Interestingly enough, not a lot of cars receive lubrication anymore, but the acronym has carried over for many years. So, when you see "LOF," that refers to an oil service. If your Service Advisor hands your car off to a tech and tells them they have a "loaf," do not think they have been told to goof off on your car.

PCM = Powertrain Control Module

The PCM is the grandfather of the computer systems on the vehicle. It is the mission control center, the head honcho, the king, the president—it is what everything else goes through. Typically, there are many computers within a single car; and they all communicate with the PCM.

TPMS = Tire Pressure Monitoring System

TPMS stands for Tire Pressure Monitoring System. Like the name says, this system monitors the tire pressure of your car. After Ford had problems with accidents caused by low air pressure on their vehicles' tires, the federal government mandated that all vehicles, beginning in 2008-2009, must contain a Tire Pressure Monitoring System.

Today, the technology actually notifies the driver when a tire has low pressure. Some systems will tell you about a specific tire—for instance, "Your left front tire is low." Some simply indicate that you have a low tire somewhere on the vehicle. Some spare tires also have these sensors—so although the four tires on the ground may be fine, you should still check the spare tire too.

TPS = Throttle Position Sensor

In the past, a car had a physical cable that connected the gas pedal with the throttle control mechanism on the engine. Today, instead of a cable, your vehicle uses a throttle position sensor, which means that your gas pedal is now an electronic sensor. So, when you depress the gas pedal, you are moving a sensor. The gas pedal sensor information is sent to the throttle position sensors, which tell the onboard computer how much gas and air to allow into the engine.

DASHBOARD: LIGHTS THAT POP UP

As you sit in the driver's seat and turn on the key, you see various lights pop up on the dashboard. But what do they mean?

First, there is a reason for the color of lights on your dashboard. These colors can be associated with the traffic lights you see when you are driving down the road.

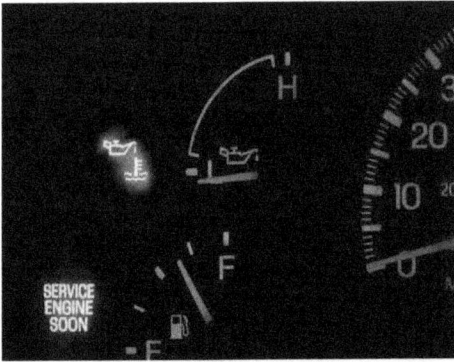

If you see a RED light, what does that usually mean to you? Stop. And when you see YELLOW? Of course, that means caution. And GREEN? Green means go.

Let's apply this to the dashboard lights. If, for example, you have the cruise control on, the button is normally some sort of orange color. Once you set the cruise control, the button turns green.

Your dashboard lights are very important. *Never ignore them.* If a red dashboard illuminates, you should discontinue driving immediately and seek service by a qualified technician right away.

ABS Light:

The ABS light relates to your brakes, as we mentioned previously. If the ABS light is on, the Anti-lock Brake System computer has found a fault somewhere in the system. It could be anything from low brake fluid to a problem with a particular wheel sensor or another component within the system.

You may remember your parents telling you that if you are on ice you should pump your brakes and not apply them hard. The ABS System uses that principle as well. The ABS system pumps your brakes ten times per second, which is something no human is able to do.

When the ABS light is illuminated, your normal braking will still operate. However, if you get into a panic stop, the anti-lock brake system will *not* take over your braking—that is, your wheels will lock up like a vehicle not equipped with anti-lock brakes. Therefore, you lose the ability to maneuver around objects in your path. Instead, momentum carries you forward and you may hit the object ahead of you.

The ABS light typically illuminates as a yellow light. It does not mean that you have to stop your car immediately, but it does indicate the system will not work until you get it resolved. It does not mean your car will not stop or that your brakes have failed completely; it only indicates that the anti-lock side of your brake system will not operate in a panic stop situation on a slick surface. Drive cautiously—as you always should—and quickly get your vehicle to a shop for testing.

Check Engine Light:

The check engine light has been around since about 1990. Initially it provided information about the emission control status of the vehicle. Check engine lights are typically orange because they still primarily deal with emission controls. However, emission controls now include additional elements, too.

Emissions concern air pollution—so, for instance, if a spark plug is not working properly, it causes the car to pollute more than it should, and the check engine light illuminates.

Formerly, a failed spark plug would not cause the check engine light to illuminate. It would come on if you had a fuel canister that was full of gasoline or if the EGR (Exhaust Gas Recirculation) system failed. Now the check engine light encompasses many things. There are somewhere between six hundred and nine hundred different reasons why the check engine light might illuminate. A technician needs to perform tests on the system to determine the actual cause so they can correct this problem.

Oil Light:

The oil light can indicate an issue with the oil level or oil pressure—or both. If the engine loses oil pressure, the oil light will illuminate. That light is red because you have to shut the engine down quickly. If the oil pressure is too low, there will be internal damage similar to driving without oil in the engine.

To clarify, you can be low on oil and still have oil pressure. The oil light may not let you know that you are low on oil—in many cars, only checking the level with a dipstick can tell you if you are low on oil. (One new technology in some of the higher end cars, like some BMW and Mercedes models, uses no dipstick. Instead, a sensor inside the engine reads the oil level and indicates its level. Most cars still have a dipstick.)

Even when you are a quart or two low on oil, you still have enough oil in the engine to produce oil pressure. In that case, the oil light might not illuminate because adequate oil pressure exists. However, the lower your oil level, the more stress and damage to your engine may occur. Potentially, you could have a low oil level and no indicator light to warn you. We encourage you to inspect your engine's oil level consistently. Your vehicle owner's manual states to check your engine oil level every time you refuel your vehicle.

Having a sufficient oil level provides several benefits. Lubricating the engine is the oil's primary job, but it also increases fuel mileage when the proper oil is used.

Oil Life Indicator Light:

The oil life indicator light displays the percentage remaining in the current oil service of the vehicle. This technology is here to stay and very accurate. This system is a statistical model measuring starting and operating cycles of the vehicle. This displays information to the driver defining how much life remains in the current. A misnomer of this system is that it displays to the driver if the oil level is low. For the record, the oil life indicator DOES NOT inform the driver if the oil level is low. Our oil service technician always measures the oil level prior to changing the oil. It is not uncommon for our advisors to report to the customer that the oil level was abnormally low. When this occurs, the customer often states, "my oil life indicator did not display the oil level was low". We then explain the oil level is NOT measured from the oil life indicator system. We always encourage our customers to monitor the oil levels. We would rather not sell a customer an engine replacement due not monitoring an oil level.

Reduced Power Light:

Reduced power is something primarily seen on GM vehicles. The reduced power light is usually red and indicates that something has gone wrong, that the vehicle has gone into "limp mode"—as in "we are limping" or "we only have one leg and cannot run." Such a fault in this system could be problematic. Many times, this fault pertains to either transmission functions or accelerating functions. If this light illuminates, you must get it in for service.

Some limp modes limit your speed to no more than 25 miles an hour, which will allow you to drive to a safe place. You will likely need to have it towed from that point, especially if you have a long way to go. Other limp modes allow you to go 40 miles per hour, usually enough that you can get to a repair facility on your own.

The reduced power light will most always be red. It indicates a problem that needs to receive immediate attention.

Smart Air Bag Light:

Almost all cars today are equipped with smart air bags. These sensors measure the weight of the person in the front passenger seat. Depending on that weight, the air bag may or may not deploy. You do not need to do anything when this light illuminates. If there is a small child in the front seat, the smart bag is aware of this information. If the weight in the front seat does not meet the minimum limit established by the manufacturer, the smart air bag light will illuminate to inform you that the airbag is off on the passenger side.

The airbag does not deploy with a child in the front passenger seat is because the car industry has learned that small children do not withstand the explosion of an airbag as well as an adult.

The inside of an airbag contains a substance similar to gunpowder. When triggered, the "gunpowder" explodes the bag out of the dash at an extremely high rate of speed. The air inside that bag immediately deflates, but is present for just long enough to provide a cushion to the blow of an impact.

Typically, the occupant of the seat moves forward while the bag deploys rearward so a collision takes place between the bag and the occupant. Because the airbag deploys at such a high rate of speed, a child's body simply cannot withstand that kind of force. Injury or death can occur as a result. After learning this, car manufacturers introduced smart bags—which was quite a "smart" thing to do.

SRS Light:

Air bags are very important elements for your safety in a vehicle. Cars equipped with air bags have an SRS light (or air bag light) on the dashboard. SRS is an acronym for Supplementary Restraint System—the key word being *supplementary.*

That means it supplements your safety system and that safety system is your seat belt. If you are not wearing your seat belt when you are in an accident that deploys the airbags, a greater amount of bodily injury will occur. For that reason, *you should ALWAYS wear your seatbelt.*

If the airbag light is illuminated, there is a problem in the system and the airbags will not deploy in an accident. As you can imagine, this can be very serious. If your SRS light illuminates, get your vehicle to the shop quickly.

Temperature Light:

Most cars today have an engine temperature gauge as well as a temperature light. The engine temperature light will always be red, indicating that you need to shut the car down as soon as possible. The longer you continue to drive, the more damage will occur. Eventually, you will damage the engine internally. By continuing to drive the vehicle you will create more problems— very costly problems.

When the temperature light illuminates, you should pull over and check the temperature gauge. If it indicates the engine is too hot, turn your vehicle off as quickly as you safely can. Then you want to determine the cause of the problem.

The first step in the troubleshooting process is to make sure that your coolant level is full. However, be very careful! We advise you to use extreme caution when checking your coolant level or adding coolant to a hot car because you can be burned. It is best to let the car sit for at least an hour with the hood raised for the engine to cool down before adding coolant. You must check the radiator coolant level as well as the cooling system reservoir/overflow bottle.

The need to add coolant usually indicates you have a leak that needs to be evaluated and repaired. If the coolant is full and the vehicle is running hot, that means that a component within the system has failed. Either way, you will need to get your car to the repair facility quickly. It is usually best towed into a shop.

Traction Control Light:

The vehicle computer not only monitors the brake system and airbags, but it also helps move power from one tire to another in all-wheel-drive vehicles. For example, in an all-wheel drive vehicle, let's say you become stuck in sand, ice, or in snow and are trying to get out. One of your wheels is usually stuck worse than the others—it is spinning but not getting any traction. The traction control system will move the power from the wheel that is spinning to a wheel that is not, since the non-spinning wheel has greater traction. The traction control system allows power to be transferred so that you can gain traction, have greater control and get out of a situation where you may normally remain stuck.

Traction control also works during acceleration. An example of acceleration mode is when the weight of the car shifts from one side to the other as you turn a corner. The traction control system moves the power to the wheels with the best traction.

The traction control light illuminates briefly whenever the system activates. If there is a failure in the system, the light will stay illuminated. That is when you need to take your vehicle in for inspection.

DASHBOARD GAUGES

Many cars have dashboard gauges in addition to dashboard lights. The following pages describe the primary gauges you will find on the dashboards of today's vehicles. These gauges provide a quick and easy way to tell how well our car is functioning.

Battery Gauge:

The battery gauge, also known as the voltage gauge, simply measures battery voltage. You will usually see a small picture of a battery on this gauge. Some gauges will have a number 12, which relates to the voltage. However, most of the time the normal position for the needle, when everything is acceptable with the battery and charging system, is in the middle of the gauge.

Fuel Gauge:

Most people know that "E" does not stand for "enough"—it stands for empty. And "F" of course stands for full.

In today's cars, the fuel pump is located *inside* the gas tank. Having enough fuel in the tank helps keep that little electric motor—called your fuel pump—cool, and will typically make it last longer.

As a rule, you should keep at least a quarter tank of fuel in your car at all times. This will add life to the fuel pump because it is an electric motor, which creates heat while running. Excessive heat shortens the life of the pump. That is why keeping enough fuel in the tank helps it last longer, especially in hot climates.

My advice is to refuel your car completely when your gauge indicates a quarter of a tank. If you always run in that quarter to empty range, you are going to shorten the life of the pump and that is an expensive repair. Not only that, but when you need to get somewhere right away, you will want more than a quarter of a tank of gas.

Odometer:

The odometer gauge tells you how many miles are on your vehicle. The accuracy of an odometer gauge has changed over the years. Today it is electronic, whereas years ago, a cable ran from the speedometer head down to the transmission, rotating with the transmission. That allowed odometer readings to be altered. That's impossible with the LED-displayed odometers we have today, which accurately show a car's mileage.

Speedometer:

The speedometer gauge is, of course, useful for showing how fast you are moving. Its speed sensors are reliable and accurate. The onboard computer also uses this information to tell the transmission when to shift.

Tachometer:

Most tachometer gauges (also called "tachs" or RPM gauges) are circular and have a series of numbers on them—often 0-8.

Even when you are sitting still, you will see the tachometer needle move around the gauge as you accelerate by pressing on the gas pedal. The tachometer indicates how many times the engine is rotating each minute.

Multiply the number on the gauge by one thousand—for example, if the needle is sitting at 1, the engine is rotating one thousand times per minute. (If the numbers on the tachometer are multiples of 10—numbers like 20, 30, 40, and so on—then you multiply that number by one hundred instead of one thousand.) That number is how many times the engine makes one full revolution each minute—called revolutions per minute or "RPMs" for short.

It can be helpful to keep an eye on the RPM gauge. The RPM number will drop each time the transmission shifts into a higher gear to increase fuel economy. If you notice that the engine appears to be running at a higher RPM than normal, it may indicate that something is not right—that the engine is working harder than usual. Another situation when the tachometer is helpful is as you are idling. If you have a vacuum leak or a similar problem, your idling RPM will be higher than usual. Most engines should run just below the 1 mark. If the idling RPM is significantly higher, that is a problem. You should expect to see the idling RPM a little bit higher when the engine is cold. Once the engine reaches operating temperature, you will see the gauge go back down to the 650-750 RPM range. Isn't understanding acronyms cool?

Temperature Gauge:
One common gauge is the cold/hot gauge, also referred to as the coolant temperature gauge.

Typically, you find the coolant temperature gauge on the left side of the dash. This gauge monitors the temperature of the engine.

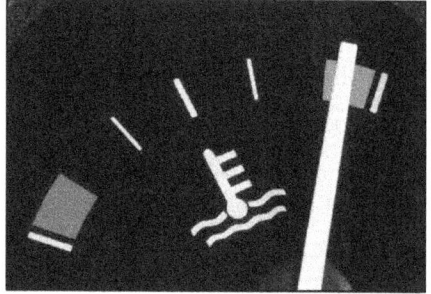

Transmissions usually will not shift into the final drive gear until the engine temperature has reached at least a quarter of the way of its full gauge range. Most gauges are set to run—in normal operation—about midway up the gauge. So, you will usually see a "C" (for cold) on the bottom and an "H" (for hot) on the top (or Blue for cold and Red for hot).

The gauge may be installed horizontally—in that case, the 'C' would be on the left and the 'H' would be on the right. Typically the needle will be in the middle of the gauge, indicating what is called, "Operating Temperature."

Interestingly, if the indicator needle indicates your engine is staying cold, that has a negative effect on your fuel mileage. The vehicle's computer is designed to put fuel in the engine based on a certain engine temperature. When the engine is cold, it puts in more fuel because a cold engine needs more. If the thermostat is not working—a typical failure—then the computer perceives that the engine is running at a colder temperature and continues putting more fuel into the engine, increasing your gasoline usage. Because the thermostat can affect fuel mileage, it is important that you are familiar with the temperature gauge to know what is normal. Check that gauge on a consistent basis. Remember: If you continue running the vehicle when the gauge shows the engine is hot, this will cause very expensive and critical internal engine damage. Too many times we have seen very expensive engine damage caused by someone who knew the gauge was reading hot but explained that they only drove "less than a mile" to get to an exit, home, or elsewhere.

NOISES

One of the greatest things about car ownership is really getting to know your car. That means using your five senses—hearing, sight, smell, taste, and touch. You can use your senses to know what is normal for *your* car so you will recognize when something has changed.

When it comes to hearing noises that you know are not normal—not what you are used to hearing—one of the best things to do is "show the noise."

When you take the car into a service facility, do not try to explain the noise. *Show* them the noise. One of the greatest helps to any service facility is when the vehicle owner pays attention so they can duplicate the noise.

- How fast was I going?
- Was I turning?

- Was I braking?
- Was I accelerating?
- What were the scenarios?
- Was I going uphill or downhill?

Pay attention to the environment and the activity that is taking place when the noise occurs. Then you can take that information, go to the repair facility, get someone in the car with you and duplicate the sound. Highly trained automotive technicians can typically hear many noises that you may not hear. This small step will assist the technician in locating and correcting the same noise that concerned you. When you pay attention to how the car normally sounds, you will recognize when something changes.

Brake Squeaking

One common noise that often scares people is a squeaky noise that happens when you push on your brake pedal. A high-pitched noise is indicative of brakes needing repair, especially if this is a new sound. Sometimes what we will call "inferior" brake pads or "inferior" parts are used on a brake job. In those cases, you should expect some squeaking.

The sound is not necessarily metal contacting metal, but actually a vibration of the brake pad against the rotor, which comes out as an audible squeak. The vibration is at a decibel level that sounds like a squeak, so this can occur due to the type of brake pad used or the surface of the rotor.

However, if you have a good brake system and use high quality parts, you should not hear any noise. If noise occurs at some point in the future, you should recognize it as a problem and have the brake system inspected for any wear, tear or other issue.

Brake Grinding

Grinding usually happens after squeaking. Some brakes never squeak, but go straight to grinding. That is typically metal grinding on metal, and you definitely need to get your vehicle into a shop.

Some of the higher end manufacturers, such as Mercedes, BMW and Lexus, have what are called "brake pad wear indicators." These are just small wires built into the brake pad. Once that wire makes contact with the rotor, a dash light comes on that says "brake wear indicator." At that point, you can bet it is time to replace your pads. Once the sensor makes contact with the rotor, the sensor is ruined and will have to be replaced along with the brake pads.

Squeaky Engine

Many times, you will find a plastic splash shield installed underneath the front of the car for multiple purposes. These shields not only prevent foreign objects from getting into the engine compartment and causing damage, but also protect against water getting into the drive belt area. If water enters that area, the drive belt may actually slip on the pulleys. You are hearing the squeaking noise because water intrusion has occurred. This is not especially harmful but it probably means that the shield is either disfigured or not there at all.

Shields are frequently damaged when you pull too close to parking spots and hit the sidewalk curb slightly, or when you hit one of those parking stops because your car sits a little bit lower than the average vehicle. If you hit the shield enough times, eventually it will come off.

If that happens, your lower engine area will be exposed and could sustain damage from water, a rock or other debris. Check to see if this plastic shield is in good condition when you wash your car or get fuel. It only takes a moment, and could save you thousands of dollars in repairs.

Thumping While Turning

Sometimes when you turn, you will hear a thumping noise and possibly feel a jerking action through the steering wheel. Several problems could cause this thumping noise.

One problem could be your "constant velocity joints" (or CV joints). Your axle has a constant velocity joint built into it that maintains quickness of motion to the wheels when you turn your steering wheel. When CV joints wear out, they cause a thumping or knocking noise when you turn. The only repair option is to replace the CV joint.

Another thumping noise involves the brakes. Usually occurring at highway speeds, you will hear this when you apply the brakes. It could be something you hear or something you feel. Many times, you see the steering wheel shake.

That usually means the rotors, which are a brake component, are warped. The rotors turn with the wheel as you drive. When you apply the brakes, the brake pads rub against the rotor to create the friction that causes your vehicle to slow down. If the surface of the rotor is not smooth or straight, it produces a thumping noise or a vibration.

Another phrase we hear is described as a "pulsation of the brakes" when they are applied. You typically hear or feel this pulsation when you brake at speeds above 45 miles per hour. You may not necessarily feel the pulsations if you are braking at 20 miles per hour, but once you get up to highway speeds and apply the brakes, you are more likely to feel or hear the vibrations.

Though not necessarily a dangerous situation, it can be quite a nuisance. It also can have a negative impact on brake pad and steering life.

Thumping While Driving

If you hear a regular thumping or vibration that varies with your speed as you are driving down the road, the tires are usually the culprits. Many times, the tread in the tire is separating internally.

Want a sure-fire way to know if this has occurred? Try this: Drive across a parking lot at 2 to 3 miles per hour, then let go of the steering wheel. If your steering wheel shakes back and forth, slightly left to right, that is an indication that the tread has moved inside the tire, and you definitely need to replace the tires.

The age at which you should replace a tire has become an issue over the years. All tires have a number on them that indicates the age of the tire. The number will start with the letters DOT (an abbreviation for Department of Transportation), followed by a series of letters and numbers. At the end of the series will be four digits. Those digits represent the week and year the tire was made. For instance, if one of your tires has the digits 4512, the tire was made in the 45th week of 2012. The numerical significance comes into play because the recommendation for replacing tires is between five and seven years old.

Check your tires. If they are 10 years old, they definitely need to be replaced. If you do not replace them, you are at a great risk of a blow out or tire separation.

Whining Engine

Whining usually occurs either from the children in the back seat or from the car's power steering pump under the hood. You will want to check both of those possibilities. You may need a cookie for one and power steering fluid for the other.

The power steering fluid is a sealed system for the most part. The fluid does not go away without cause. If you need to add power steering fluid, you most likely have a leak somewhere in the system. Adding fluid will be a temporary measure. If you have a leak, the whine may stop for a while, but once the fluid leaks out again, the whining noise will resume. Take your car for servicing if you suspect a power steering fluid leak.

Vehicle Starting

When you start your car, several noises may be heard. One is a tapping noise that can indicate that your oil is not getting where it needs to be. That noise occurs because some areas of the car need to have oil immediately upon starting. One reason some of the manufacturers have gone to a lighter weight oil is because it can get to those areas that need lubrication quicker on start-up.

Another noise you might hear is a rattling. Any time you hear a rattle in your engine when you start your car, it is metal-to-metal contact. While it will not cause *immediate* failure, problems will happen eventually. The cause is usually a low oil level, low oil pressure, or it could signal that internal wear has occurred.

ENGINE OIL

Here are some common questions about engine oil:

- *Does the type of engine oil I use really matter?*
- *Can I change the brand of oil I use?*
- *What do the numbers mean?*

All oil today is called "paraffin-based oil." That means the oil has the ability to capture dirt—this is one of its jobs. When we perform an oil service, we drain the oil from the vehicle and dirt goes with it.

Manufacturers have made changes to the oil for use in lubricating their specific engines. The car industry used to recommend oil based on geographic conditions. If you lived in a cold climate, like Alaska, thinner winter oil was recommended. If you lived in the warmer southern states, heavier oil was recommended.

All that has changed due to the tolerances built into cars by the manufacturers. Today it is more important than ever that you pay attention to the type of oil the manufacturer recommends.

The label on a bottle of oil provides information about that oil. Most people examine the weight of the oil first. Is it 5W-30? 10W-30? Or 5W-20? What does that even mean? Well, the "W" stands for winter. If we used 5W-30 for example, the "5" and "30" actually measure the thickness, or viscosity, of the oil at different temperatures.

If an oil bottle has "5W-30" on it, the oil will have a viscosity of a "5" weight oil when cold and a viscosity of a "30" weight oil when hot. This combination provides an oil that flows well at low temperatures, but still protects the engine at high temperatures. For comparison's sake, SAE 5W-30 and SAE 0W-30 will flow better at even lower temperatures than 10W-30, while still providing protection at high temperatures. Just remember, the "W" stands for winter.

Most cars today use either 5W-20 or 5W-30, regardless of geographic location. The brand you choose is up to you. Contrary to what your grandfather told you, it is okay to switch brands.

Oil service Frequency

How often you should change your oil is becoming an issue in our industry because of changes in service intervals. Years ago, it was every three months or three thousand miles. Our fathers, grandfathers and great-grandfathers all taught us that. The reason the oil needed changing so often was because the engines were exposed to the elements, and the filtering system of air and fuel was not what it is today. Your oil could be easily contaminated and cause internal engine damage. That is why car engines used to last only about fifty thousand miles.

Several things have changed since then. With the advent of electronic fuel injection, the problem with outside elements getting to the crankcase was virtually eliminated because the fuel systems are sealed. Fuel is managed better, too, so your oil is not contaminated with fuel the way it used to be.

Thus, we have better control of outside elements, like dirt and dust, coming into the engine, and we have better control through better filtering. We have better control of the amount of fuel that is dumped into an engine for burning—almost all of it is being burned these days. And finally, the oil has gotten better at suspending the dirt in the engine. When you put these factors together, your service interval can now be longer than it used to be. Some manufacturers will tell you 7,500 miles, some 10,000 miles, and some 15,000 miles. At Beachlers, we recommend oil service every 5,000 miles. To help simplify things, many cars today have oil life monitors that tell you when it is time to change your oil. We educate our customers that the oil life indicators are very accurate, and they are advised to change their oil when the indicator reads to do so. However, this does not relieve the customer from checking the oil level regularly. A common misunderstanding is that the oil life indicator monitors the oil level in the engine. This is not true, as the oil life indicator monitors only the condition of the oil, not the quantity. There is a separate system for monitoring oil level.

CHAPTER

6

CAR CARE 201

In this section, let's explore some of the more advanced areas of your vehicle, including when to buy a new one. This could become a reference manual for you and a great training manual for new drivers in your family. I have structured this section in the form of a Question and Answer series, much like the FAQ section of a website or resource book.

SHOULD YOU BUY A NEW CAR?

Let's discuss a few of the most frequently asked questions related to purchasing a new vehicle. Having this information could save you thousands of dollars.

Q. When do I need to buy a new car versus investing in the one I have?

A. Every car has a point of diminishing returns. What you do from the day you drive your car off the showroom floor and whether you think of your vehicle as an investment or as an expense affects the decisions you make about replacing it.

You should not simply say, "Well, I do not want to put that much money into my car," without doing a cost comparison. If you have properly maintained your vehicle, you should expect to get 200,000 to 400,000 miles from it. When you purchase a vehicle, it is necessary to understand that how you maintain and operate it today will determine its condition tomorrow. With proper servicing, your point of diminishing returns will be farther down the road than if you neglect your vehicle.

I have seen vehicles with as few as 75,000 miles need an engine (between $4,000 and $7,000) simply because the oil level was not monitored on a regular basis. In a case like this, investing in the repair would only be worthwhile for an extremely expensive vehicle. Otherwise, it would be time to purchase a replacement and the trade-in or resale value of the vehicle that needed a new engine would be very low. The owner's original investment would be essentially worthless.

It is always better to maintain a car correctly from the beginning so that the point of diminishing returns is much farther out than it otherwise would be.

Let's say you have a six or seven-year-old vehicle. Perhaps it needs a timing belt, or has blown a head gasket. It will cost $1,500 to $2,500 to repair a vehicle you have been driving for six to seven years. You are just not sure you want to pay that much to get it fixed, so you consider buying a new car. Here's a calculation that may help you decide.

Larry Burkett was a well-known financial advisor who started Crown Financial Ministries. He would tell you that the cheapest car you will ever own is the one in your driveway. What he means is that by having the car maintained and keeping everything in good working order, you will spend less money than purchasing a newer vehicle.

When we talk about making a major repair on a car, a way you can try to crunch the numbers is to ask yourself, "What is it going to cost me over the next year?" Let's say

BEACHLERS GUIDE TO VEHICLE CARE AND REPAIR

you need $3,000 worth of work done on your vehicle and you have decided you are not going to repair it. Instead, you are going to go buy a used vehicle.

Even if you bought an inexpensive one, around $10,000, there's still the down payment, then the calculated monthly payments if you finance. Of course, depending on the state, you might also have to pay sales tax on that vehicle. Plus, you will need to figure an almost immediate depreciation, as well. You may have personal property taxes on your vehicles, and that will increase. Your insurance will increase because, if you finance the car, you will have to have full coverage insurance. Even if you do not finance, your "new" car is typically more valuable than the one you are replacing, so your insurance rates will rise for that reason. Calculate your total cost over the next 12 months for that used car and compare that to the cost of making repairs on the one in your driveway. Can you beat the $3,000 investment in your current car?

If you apply this same principle to buying a brand new car, these dollar figures are going to increase exponentially. Therefore, it usually makes more sense to repair your existing vehicle than to buy a new one.

EXTENDED WARRANTIES

Q: If I buy a new vehicle, should I purchase an extended warranty?

A: I advise my customers against purchasing extended warranties. Evidence proves that, in most cases, the cost of the warranty is far more than the benefit received. Consumer Reports researched extended warranties. The results were, for every $1,000 dollars a consumer spends on a warranty, they receive an average of $700 in return. Not so great odds!

Note: If you're interested in learning more about this topic, see Appendix I in the back of this book.

CARING FOR YOUR CAR

Q. When should I jump-start my car?

A. The purpose of a battery is to send power to the starter, which then starts the engine. If a problem with the battery exists, it will show up when you try to start the car, not while you are driving.

We have all experienced a dead battery, haven't we? We turn the key and either hear nothing or series of repetitive clicks. The engine does not turn over. That is the only time you should jump-start your car.

If you are driving down the road and your car dies, the battery is not the cause of your car dying. Do not jump-start your car in this situation. It will not help.

Note: See the "*How-To*" Section to learn the proper way to jump-start your car.

PREMIUM FUEL

Q. Do I need to buy premium fuel?

A. The best way to determine if premium fuel is right for you is to check your owner's manual to see what they recommend for your specific car. Higher-end models may require premium gas. Those cars are designed to burn fuel at optimum levels. Both the way the engine is timed and tuned, and the type of spark plugs used ensures that when you use this fuel, you will get the optimum performance from your vehicle.

There is nothing wrong with using fuel rated at 87 octane if a higher octane fuel is not advised by the manufacturer. Components called "knock sensors" were added to vehicles a few years ago. These sensors adjust the timing if the engine begins to "ping" or "knock" due to lower octane or other factors in the fuel.

So do you have to use premium fuel? The answer is no. However, if you want the best performance for your particular vehicle, then I would recommend using the higher-grade gasoline.

MOTOR CLUB MEMBERSHIPS

Q. How beneficial are motor club memberships?

A. Motor clubs provide good benefits for the consumer and offer peace of mind for the consumer who travels often or has a loved one living away from home. Undoubtedly, their primary focus is the customer. I am thinking of clubs like AAA Motor Club or Cross Country Motor Club, the two big wheels in the industry.

It is easy to feel vulnerable when traveling through an unfamiliar part of the country. These clubs help locate a reliable repair facility, a towing company, a hotel, and other needed services for a vehicle breakdown. Therefore, you have more confidence in the support and quality service you may need.

CHAPTER

7

INTRODUCTION TO MAINTENANCE

What do we mean when we say, "maintenance?" It is a term that applies to any number of industries and essentially means the same thing in each—it means *care* or *upkeep*.

We have already discussed crucial factors in the care and upkeep of your vehicle—things such as engine oils and the benefits of regular services and inspections. Let's address a few other important components of your car's maintenance.

VEHICLE FLUIDS

Transmission Fluid

In the section on motor oil, we explained that dirt is suspended in your oil. At each oil service, the oil (and the dirt it holds) drains out of your car and is replaced by clean oil. Can we apply the same reasoning with transmissions?

Transmissions do not pull in air, but they do have metal-to-metal contact, or the potential for metal-to-metal contact (this is true with every component on your car where fluids are involved). Furthermore, transmissions are exposed to heat.

Heat plus metal-to-metal contact eventually breaks down the fluid that circulates through the system. The good news is that we do not have to service the transmission every 5,000 miles. If you are using your vehicle for towing and/or you are in a severe climate, please follow the factory specified maintenance in your owner's manual. This towing/severe climate schedule will require more frequent exchanges of transmission fluid. If you are not towing and are located in a normal climate, again, it is acceptable to adhere to the factory specified maintenance in your owner's manual. This interval will typically be much longer than the severe climate/towing schedule.

Differential Fluid

We can apply this same concept to the differential fluid. On most front-wheel-drive vehicles, the differential is a part of the transmission. The differential on rear-wheel-drive cars is located in the rear axle. Differentials also need occasional fluid changes. Your owner's manual provides the proper interval.

Power Steering Fluid

We simply recommend inspecting the power steering fluid levels regularly. As for the fluid changes, we advise adhering to the owner's manual. Most manufacturers do not require changing of the power steering fluid.

Brake Fluid

Brake fluid is a hydraulic fluid crucial to proper braking. For most domestic vehicles, no flushing of brake fluid is recommended. For other makes, the owner's manual will provide the proper interval for service.

If brake fluid must be added, it is important to use fluid that has been kept in an airtight container. Brake fluid is hygroscopic, as it is designed to absorb moisture in the brake system to prevent deterioration of the metal components. If the fluid container is left open, the fluid will absorb moisture and no longer provide protection.

Cooling System Fluid: Antifreeze/Coolant

The cooling system's primary component is antifreeze/coolant. A properly mixed coolant has protection down to -35 degrees. This in turn prevents the engine block from freezing. This coolant also helps keep the engine cool in the summer.

Coolant should be exchanged according to your factory specified maintenance in your owner's manual.

Air Conditioning System Fluids/Refrigerant

In states with sweltering, hot summers, few things are more frustrating than having your air conditioning produce hot air. Proper maintenance can prevent this.

Your air conditioning system is sealed. We know from previous discussions that in closed systems, the only way you lose fluid-- or in this case refrigerant, a gas, -is by having a leak in the system. Having the air conditioning inspected annually is a simple and wise procedure.

The air conditioning system uses oil, which is carried throughout the system by the refrigerant. Lack of oil in the system can lead to mechanical failures. Just like running your engine without oil, running your air conditioning system without proper lubrication will damage your air conditioning "engine," (also known as the compressor).

Some compressors look like very small engines on the inside. They have some of the same components as your car's engine—pistons, rings, rods and a crankshaft—only much smaller. Keeping the compressor well lubricated extends its longevity.

You should *always* have your air conditioning system serviced by an ASE Certified Technician. It is just too risky to do it yourself. Keeping your air conditioning system serviced when necessary is a great way to save money and stay cool in the heat of summer.

> **NEVER attempt to recharge your air conditioning system yourself!**

TESTING AND DIAGNOSIS

Years ago, a technician might spend five minutes diagnosing a car and five hours making the repair. Today, we might spend five hours running tests and diagnosing the vehicle, and five minutes repairing or installing a component in the vehicle. The increased use of electronics drives this change.

Vehicles today have a tremendous number of electronic systems. It is not unusual to find between five and fifteen computers on any given car. It is imperative all those computers communicate with each other. And the main computer is the Power Train Control Module. All other computers must communicate with this "mission control center" through a CAN—Controlled Area Network. Investigating these various computer systems can become complex.

Again, this is where experienced, certified technicians are worth their weight in gold. In order to repair a vehicle, it is important to know how it works. Let the professionals do their jobs—taking care of your vehicle's needs.

CHAPTER

8

CAR CARE 301

No book like this would be complete without a "How To" section. There are many things on a car that you can do yourself, and in this section, I want to discuss the proper way to do them.

YOUR AUTOMOTIVE "HOW TO" GUIDE

How to Change a Flat Tire

Most vehicles have a tire pressure monitoring system that will indicate that you have a low tire. Technology has improved to the point that some cars even indicate which tire is low, so pay attention to your dash lights. If that light illuminates, you need to quickly find a safe place to investigate the situation.

Tires can go flat over a short *or* a long period, depending on the size of the leak. When you need to change a tire, the most dangerous place for you to change it is on the side of the interstate. If possible, get off the interstate, even if that means driving on the shoulder at a very slow speed until you can exit—or at least to an area of the road where you can safely pull off the road (which to me is at least 10 to 15 feet from the edge of the freeway). Ideally, you want to exit and get to a safe location out of sight of the interstate, where you can raise the car using the tools provided. A lighted area is preferable if this occurs at night

If you have never changed a flat before, let me encourage you to practice doing so in the safety and comfort of your garage or driveway. Become familiar with the tools and the procedure. Follow the directions given in the owner's manual. If you have children of or near driving age, demonstrate the technique to them and then let them duplicate the process. The last thing you want to do is figure out how to change a flat when you are pulled off the side of a road!

The owner's manual will tell you the exact location where you must place the jack in order to raise the vehicle safely. You can damage your car, or injure yourself, if you place it incorrectly. Here is another little hint: Always loosen (but do not remove) the lug nuts holding the wheel in place *before* you hoist the car. It is much easier to remove the tire if you follow this tip.

When installing the spare tire, be sure to start each of the wheel nuts by hand. Remember to put the beveled edge of the lug nut toward the wheel. Then, with your tire iron, tighten them in a star pattern. To do this, tighten one, then skip one, tighten one, then skip one. Eventually, all wheel nuts will be tight.

> **Note:** Tighten the wheel nuts as best you can with the wheel off the ground. Then you can lower the jack completely and re-tighten in the star pattern with the wheel firmly on the ground.

Most cars come with the lug wrench you use to tighten the wheel nuts. To make it easier to change the tire, position the wrench in such a way that you can stand on it, using your leg and body weight to loosen each wheel nut if necessary. However, you do not want to do that while tightening the wheel nuts (because you can over-tighten them). After tightening all of the lug nuts, drive 50 to 100 miles, and then check them again to make certain they remain tight.

HOW TO JUMP-START A CAR

Jump-starting a car is actually controlling a spark. You are running an electrical current from one battery to another. That gives you two batteries with the potential to vent acid gas. Therefore, a controlled spark of electricity reduces the risk of injury and/or damage.

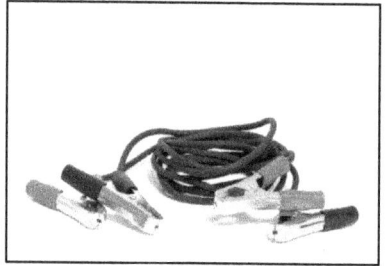

What we mean by "venting" is that it is not uncommon for battery fumes from the acid inside to slowly leak from the top of the battery. Since the acid gases can be explosive, you could potentially blow up the battery if you do not control that spark. And if your face happens to be in the vicinity at the time, bad things could occur. If you have safety glasses, it would be a good idea to wear them when you jump-start a car. Safety glasses are about $1.50 at most places.

Here is the right way to jump-start a car:

Note: The car with the "good" battery should *not* be running at this point.

1. Connect the red jumper cable clamp to the positive terminal (+) of the "good" battery.

2. Connect the other end of that red cable to the positive terminal of the "bad" battery.

3. Connect the black cable clamp to the negative (-) terminal of the "good" battery.

4. Connect the final cable clamp to a good solid metal surface under the hood of the car being "jumped," such as a bracket or other metal object. If necessary, you can attach to the negative terminal of the battery; it is just not as safe. (Hint: the positive battery terminal is slightly larger than the negative battery terminal.

5. Have the driver of the "good" car start the engine and run at just above idle for a couple of minutes.

6. Then, attempt to start the car with the dead battery. If done correctly and the problem is just a dead battery, the car should start immediately.

7. Carefully remove the cables in reverse order.

Jump-starting a car essentially uses electricity from the good battery to power the bad one, thus making an electrical circuit. Making the last connection to a major metal part on the engine instead of the battery will minimize the possibility of an uncontrolled spark, thus keeping you and your battery safe.

Jump Starting a Car: Illustration
Good Battery   "Dead/Bad" Battery

Connect Positive to Positive

THEN

Connect Negative to Negative
(or to solid metal surface)

When jump-starting a car, remember:

+ to + THEN – to –

HOW TO MANAGE A BREAKDOWN

You should be familiar enough with your gauges to know what "normal" is, so when the gauges are not within normal range, you will realize something is wrong.

When you are driving, and begin to feel something about the function of your car that you are unsure about, or hear a new noise, cautiously move into the right lane. You do *not* want your vehicle to be disabled in the left lane or in the median of a freeway. Always try to get to a safe location to manage a breakdown.

If your vehicle begins to overheat, the gauges will indicate it, so monitor them closely. If your vehicle *is* overheating, turn the engine off as soon as possible.

The second thing you should do during a breakdown is to make a call. These days most people carry cell phones. I recommend you keep numbers for a towing company, motor club or repair shop in your phone for such an emergency.

Make sure you are in a safe spot and keep passengers a safe distance from the highway while you wait for help to arrive. This will decrease your risk of an accident. Managing a breakdown, though sometimes nerve-racking and always inconvenient, is not that complicated. Try to remember the following:

1. Do not panic!
2. Think "safety."
3. Call for assistance.

HOW TO MANAGE AN ACCIDENT

Having an accident is always an emotional situation— whether that emotion is anger, frustration, fear, sorrow, anxiety, worry or panic. Even something as minor as a fender-bender or a slow-speed parking lot accident can be enough to create emotion. Try to remain calm.

When you are in an accident, remember first that insurance companies typically investigate accidents to determine fault, so do not assume or admit that you are the guilty party. Being in an emotional state or in a state of shock can skew your perception of the accident. Let them do their job.

Next, call the police. Once they are on their way, exchange insurance information with the other driver. You probably do not need to worry about writing any information down—just use your cell phone to take pictures of their driver's license, their car and the area. (It will not hurt to take a picture of the driver, too, if you can do so safely.) Make sure you get proof of insurance from the other driver. If they have the necessary information available at the scene, call immediately to verify their coverage. Just because the paper says they are covered does not mean they are. You should have your insurance information in the glove compartment to give the other party.

For most states, unless there is bodily injury, you should remove the vehicle from the road. You can be ticketed for obstruction of traffic if you keep your car on the road when there is no personal injury. Remove your car to a safe place and proceed to work out the details with the other party as you await the arrival of the police.

Tow trucks dispatched by the police are often under contract with the police. Typically, they will tow your vehicle to their lot and charge you storage fees while it is there. These fees can mount up quickly, especially if there is a dispute with your insurance company regarding your claim and your vehicle can't be repaired right away.

You have the option of having your vehicle towed to a collision repair facility of your choosing. Most collision repair facilities allow cars to remain there, free of charge, while the insurance company details are resolved. This can save you a significant amount of money in storage fees.

It is a good idea to think ahead and be prepared. Know where you want your car towed if you should have an accident. If your car care shop does not do body work, ask them to recommend someone you can trust, and keep their phone number and address in your smart phone or glove box, along with your insurance information.

How to Manage Being Stuck in Traffic

The one thing you want to avoid is becoming trapped behind the car in front of you. The way I avoid that is to stop far enough behind a vehicle that I can still see their rear tires touching the pavement. That way, I can maneuver around it if I need to.

You have heard of, or perhaps have been a part of, a pile up where one car rams into the car in front of them and it causes a domino effect. If you leave enough space between you and the car in front of you, you are not trapped; you can swing your car to either side and avoid being rammed from behind.

Sometimes traffic jams simply cannot be avoided. That is another reason to keep more than a quarter tank of gas in your car. You do not want to run out of fuel at this time.

Always watch your temperature gauge when you are stopped in traffic. Most cars are designed to be able to idle indefinitely—even with the air conditioning on. Still, you need to watch that gauge. If you notice your engine heating up, roll your windows down and turn off the air conditioning.

Traffic jams occur in the winter, as well. Some states require you to have a safety kit in your vehicle. The kit usually contains items like bottled water, a blanket and a flashlight. It is an excellent idea. You never know when you will be caught in traffic, or how long it will take to clear the roads.

HOW TO DRIVE ON SNOW AND ICE

Snow and ice certainly provide challenges to drivers. When driving on snow you need increased traction. That is why four-wheel-drive vehicles (or front-wheel-drive vehicles) maneuver better in the snow—simply because of their superior traction due mainly to the weight of the engine and transmission on the front wheels. Nothing helps on ice. My best advice is to simply stay put, if at all possible, and avoid driving on icy roads. If that is not possible, keep your speed low, try to anticipate trouble, and follow the instructions below for driving on snow.

In deep snow, one tip that might come in handy is to lower the air pressure in your tires to about 25 pounds of pressure. You still will not be able to drive fast, but since there is more rubber on the road, you will notice an improvement in your ability to negotiate snowy road conditions.

We learned years ago to gently pump the brakes in the snow, but the best advice I can offer is to drive as though you had an egg under the gas and brake pedals. Accelerate slowly and brake gently. Do not push on the pedals too strongly. You will break the eggs!

Also when braking, it is a wise idea to position the gear shift into neutral. This will eliminate the "drag" from the transmission at the drive wheels. This will slightly improve your braking ability in ice or snow.

How to Buy a Used Car

Buying a used car can be risky business. Let me offer some strategies that might prove helpful in that situation.

First, do your homework. Review online, read consumer magazines, peruse some used car lots, investigate the "For Sale" ads in your newspaper and check out *Kelly Blue Book (www.kbb.com)* for reasonable pricing. Take all the time you need to figure out exactly what you are interested in—make, model and even options.

Once you have narrowed your search, it is time to find that perfect vehicle—whether you intend to buy from an individual or a car dealership. Study the car, walk around it and look at it from different angles. Once you finish assessing the cosmetic aspects, then sit behind the steering wheel. Touch everything you can touch. Check out the wipers, the radio, the heat and air, the glove box and the lights. Make certain everything works, including turn signals, power windows, power locks, power seats, rear wipers, and so on.

If everything checks out, let the seller know you would like to take about 30 to 45 minutes to road test this vehicle. If they want to ride with you, great. Make certain they are willing for you to spend the time you need.

Most people drive the car around the block or spend ten minutes driving up the road and back and say, "I will take it"—but not you. You are too savvy. During your test drive, listen to the vehicle. Notice the way it feels, handles, and steers. You do not have to be an automotive mechanic to know if something is not quite right.

If you hear a noise that concerns you, or there is a shake or shimmy in the steering, or anything else that do not quite seem right, then make note of it. Spend time driving both city and interstate speeds. See how the vehicle handles corners, decelerates, brakes, and accelerates—just as you would drive the vehicle on any given day.

Use your senses. Do not play the radio. Make sure the radio plays, then turn it off and listen. Use your five senses to note if anything seems abnormal.

If everything checks out, move to the next step—take it to an ASE-certified technician for a used-car inspection. A trained technician will inspect the exterior and interior of the car, perform a vehicle road test, and then complete the inspection on the hoist. The technician follows a detailed inspection form to cover most aspects of a vehicle.

Never purchase a used vehicle until after the shop you trust has performed a pre-purchase inspection. If the person you are buying from does not want to allow you to take the car to a shop, then walk away. There is a reason for it.

Of course, we may find the vehicle you are considering is in great shape. And when you get an "all clear" from someone who truly knows what they are doing, it will give you great confidence. In most cases, some work is needed, though. Through this process, the ASE-certified technician can help you make a decision about repairs that may need to be completed now or in the near future. We can also inform you of the costs of repairs.

That will give you greater wisdom and leverage in making an offer to the seller. Once you decide to buy this particular vehicle, you are ready for the final step—making the deal.

You should not talk about price, or make any offer until you have taken all these steps. Then you will be able to approach the seller and tell them, "I would like to buy this car. I have had it inspected and here is the estimate of the items that need attention before I consider it to be in satisfactory condition. With that in mind, I am willing to pay this amount for it—and if that is agreeable with you, I am ready to buy it today."

That is the right way to buy a vehicle. Constrain your emotions, have a certified technician inspect it and know what you are getting into before you make an offer. By following this process, you will save yourself from some unpleasant surprises that could cost you a lot of money.

HOW TO FIND A GOOD REPAIR SHOP

If you are moving out of your current area, one of the best actions you could take in finding a reliable new repair shop is to ask your current one. Most shops are in some kind of network or association and may know a good shop in the area where you are relocating.

If you are looking for a reliable repair shop in your current locale, here are some tips to find a satisfactory facility. Do some investigation. Ask others if they are satisfied with their shops. Check with your local Better Business Bureau.

When you have narrowed down your choices, move to the next step. Make an appointment for something relatively simple and easy—a tire rotation, or an oil service. When you take your car in, tell them you will wait for it. While you are waiting, look and listen. You can learn much by this simple process.

While service is being performed, pay attention to how employees interact with each other and with the other customers. Notice how they answer the phone. If possible, watch the way they care for your vehicle. It will not take long before you arrive at an opinion about how professionally they operate their shop. This can go a long way in helping you make a decision.

Find out whether their technicians are ASE-certified and if they are required to participate in continuing education/training. Ascertain to what extent they service your particular make and model. Do they have the software to communicate with the computer systems on your vehicle? Do they have the specialized tools your car may require?

Ask them if they utilize any system of reminders to inform you when it is time for service. Do they follow factory specified maintenance to reduce your cost per mile and best extend the life of the vehicle?

Compare the shops you visit. Make an informed decision and choose the one that best meets your needs.

Five Questions to Ask a Shop

If you are not able to visit the repair shop, a phone call may need to suffice. If so, here are five simple questions you can ask any shop. (As a word of caution, let me say that it's extremely dangerous to choose a shop based on their pricing. There is too much room for misunderstanding and manipulation if price is your only criteria.) That is why I advise you to ask these questions and compare the answers you receive:

1. What is your warranty?
2. What is the average turn around time on a vehicle repair?
3. Are your technicians ASE-Certified and do you have any ASE Master Technicians?
4. Do you provide customer transportation?
5. What happens if I have trouble when you are closed?

These five simple questions will successfully point you to the best shop in your area.

I

APPENDIX I: EXTENDED WARRANTIES

First, extended warranty prices vary greatly. A dealership typically offers two types. One is the type the manufacturer offers, so if I bought a Subaru, it would be a Subaru extended warranty. If I bought a GM, it would be a GM extended warranty. The dealership also offers an "after-market extended warranty." That is usually serviced by a company whose sole product is extended warranties.

For whatever reason, most after-market extended warranty companies are located or originated in the St. Louis area. The St. Louis Better Business Bureau and the St. Louis Attorney General spend significant time dealing with these companies because of consumer complaints.

ConsumerAffairs.com says, "From what we have heard, we suspect that most extended warranties are a waste of money that could be better spent on performing exquisite maintenance, still the best insurance of trouble-free motoring." They also said, "Sixty-five percent (or more than 8,000) *Consumer Reports* readers surveyed by the Consumer Reports National Research Center in the winter of 2011 said they spent significantly more

for a new car warranty than they got back in repair cost savings."
That is very common. (This information is taken from an article
located at: *http://www.consumeraffairs.com/news04/2005/
extended_warranty.html*)

There are even conventions for these companies that teach
how to sell an extended warranty. The following information is
from the website, *WarrantyInnovations.com*. The whole purpose
of the convention, throughout all their breakout sessions and
their main course, was this—and this is in the notes of the
meeting!

"The discussion will also include ways to leverage
systems and data to drive extended warranty sales, how to build
a recurring revenue stream with extended warranties in
maintenance, lower costs, and claims against your program and
how to better work with your insurance and our administrator."

That information clearly states that their intent is to sell
more warranties and reduce the number of claims. Extended
warranties are a contract, and I learned a long time ago that
contracts are usually written in favor of those who write them.

Without question, extended warranty contracts are not
good for the consumer. Can you find people who have been able
to save money in buying an extended warranty? Yes, you can.
The response rate, according to *Consumer Reports,* is about one
in five—so about 20% said they had a net savings.

The *Consumer Reports* study basically says that when you are buying a car, it is better *not* to buy an extended warranty, but instead use those dollars to maintain your vehicle. In the survey, respondents cited warranty costs of $1,000 on average that provided benefits of $700—a $300 loss. Forty-two percent of extended warranties were never used, and only about a third of all respondents used their plan to cover a serious problem.

There are also exclusions from coverage by an extended warranty. So, even though you purchased the warranty, it will still be necessary to pay for repairs that are not covered. Beware, because there is a large amount of fine print in those contracts. Read it carefully if you are considering purchasing a warranty.

Most extended warranties give the warranty company the option of installing used parts on your car. So if your transmission fails, instead of getting a new transmission, you may receive a used one—one out of a salvage yard or from a recycler. It is their choice, not yours. That is scary. However, it saves the warranty company money.

All in all, it is really pretty simple. The warranty companies have to make a profit to stay in business, they have considerable overhead such as personnel, buildings, office infrastructure, advertising, etc. This requires that overall they take in far more money than they spend on repairs. As a total group, the consumer loses. They need to, or the company would fail.

www.Beachlers.com

II

APPENDIX II: FUEL TIPS AND TALES

We also sell fuel, which is a major expense in operating a vehicle, so I would like to give you some advice and information about that cost. You can reduce some of your fuel costs yourself, while other cost components involve issues that you may want to be aware of, especially at election time.

What you drive, how you drive, and how much you drive are factors behind your fuel bill. If you can get by without a large vehicle, you will save money. Performing regular maintenance of all systems will keep your vehicle running efficiently so less fuel is required. Quick starts and high speed (above 65 mph) use considerably more fuel, so lighten up on the pedal! It is also smart to coast sometimes—you do not have to drive the speed limit all the way to the red light and then slam on your brakes. The obvious way to save gas is to not turn the key. Combine trips and carpool to avoid a trip entirely.

A variety of taxes go into the fuel price, but to get your attention, the fuel taxes collected at our location in 2014 totaled $817,835. Included in this are the federal motor fuel tax, the state motor fuel tax, the City of Peoria motor fuel tax, an underground storage tank tax, and the sales taxes for the city, county, and state. The federal motor fuel tax is probably the fairest of any tax in our system since most of it is spent on roads and highways.

The state and local sales taxes are charged on the base price of gas plus other taxes (except the state motor fuel tax), so the sales taxes increase when gas prices increase; they are not a set per-gallon amount. Neighboring states either, do not charge sales tax on fuel or it is at a lower rate, and the local governments do not have a sales tax on fuel. This causes Illinois to have higher gas prices than surrounding states, a definite challenge in selling fuel at the border.

Ethanol is in our fuel because of tax subsidies. This is unfortunate for consumers for two reasons: 10% ethanol in gas reduces gas mileage by 3%, and the producers of ethanol and oil companies are receiving money that would have been paid in sales tax that could benefit the residents. To compensate for the higher cost of ethanol, sales taxes are reduced by 20% and the federal motor fuel tax is reduced by 5.4¢ per gallon. I suspect that city and county governments are not aware of how this policy affects their tax collections. Because ethanol production consumes 1.3 units of energy for every unit produced, it is not a promising investment for the taxpayer.

With the high cost and dramatic fluctuations in gas prices, some feel that there must be huge, unscrupulous profits in the system. First, I would like to note that gasoline prices have not outpaced inflation. We have a photo in our customer waiting area with Bob Beachler pumping gas in 1955. The price on the pump was 32.9 cents, and at that time postage for a first class letter was 3 cents. Second, if the oil companies are making a killing, you can participate by buying stock. As for us as a dealer, when we buy gas for $3.22/gallon including all taxes ($2.61 without taxes, as of October, 2014), our selling price is $3.26/gallon. That is a gross—not net—profit of just 4.0¢ per gallon if a bankcard is used. Other dealers in the area influence our price, but in most cases, large companies competing in a free market determine their price.

ABOUT THE AUTHOR

Brett Beachler was raised in Peoria, Illinois, and spent his time around cars as he grew up. He graduated from Bradley University with a degree in business in 1993, and after working for a large, multi-state corporation for four years, rejoined the family business in 1998.

Brett and daughter Katie

Brett enjoys spending time with his wife and five children, four of whom are out of the family home and in college.

When time allows, he is active in mountain biking, road biking, cross-country skiing, and running. Brett enjoys reading, with special interest in books related to the gospel or business.